Dr. Ebony Presents

Food is Not Bae

A guide to ending your toxic

relationship with food

Ebony O. Butler, PhD

Dr. Ebony Presents Food is Not Bae: A Guide to Ending Your Toxic
Relationship with Food

Ebony Butler, PhD

Co-founder & CEO of My Sister's Keep-her, LLC

My Sister's Keep-her, LLC

drebonyonline@gmail.com

www.mysisterskeep-her.com

Food Is Not Bae

Ordering information

Special discounts are available on quantity purchases by corporations, associations, and others. For details, contact the publisher at the email address provided above.

Published by Dr. Ebony & My Sister's Keep-her

Printed in USA

ISBN-13: 978-1979878401
ISBN-10: 1979878404

DEDICATED TO

This book is dedicated my mother, Jessie Burrell, and sister, Rhoda Ratliff (Kesha). Mama, without your limitless love and support, I wouldn't know that there are no limits to what I dream and DO. Kesha, thank you for being by business partner and friend! Thank you for teaching me what you know. It's because of your selflessness that I have a passion for learning and teaching. You ladies inspire me. This book is also dedicated to all of those women who see more to life than their current circumstances. That's the spirit in all of us that knows that where we are now is not the end of the story. We still have many more chapters to write!

ACKNOWLEDGMENT

Thank you to all of the women we've had the privilege of working with and who have trusted us with your journey. You all give me strength and help me to keep walking in my purpose. Thank you, Dawniel Winningham, for your early stages of business coaching! We talked about this book, and I finally did it! Thank you to a very special couple and my business BFFs, Brent & Angel Rhodes of Marriage of God. Thank you both for pushing me to stop talking about it and to starting doing! Thank you to Mr. Felix Anderson for helping me to wake my successful self up! Thank you for your heart to see your people win and pouring knowledge into this process. And, last but not least, thank you to my life partner, Jamila. Thank you for your support since Day 1. Thank you for putting up with the constant attachment to my phone! Thank you for your love and friendship. I love you!

TABLE OF CONTENT

Preface

When I was growing up, the most important relationships I developed were with the people in my immediate family. My family network consisted of my mom who made single parenting look easy, aunts who helped her raise me, uncles who were comedians of the family, cousins who were my first best friends, and a bunch of good times...many of which were centered around FOOD! It didn't take long for me to build the expectation that if we were getting together as a family, there would be food! Consequently, as my relationships with other people shaped so did my relationship with food. I began to associate good food with good times, primarily as it related to my family gatherings. When there was a celebration, we ate. When all of the cousins were together, we ate. When there was death in the family, we ate. When someone didn't feel well, you fed them. When people visited your home, you fed them. We bonded around food. And, even more significant, strong holds were being made *with* food.

My story isn't unique in that a lot of my earlier memories and emotional experiences were centered around food, which is common across many families, cultures, and traditions. Food is the thread that holds families and personal relationships together. However, because this is common, does not mean that it was OK. Many bonds and relationships that people build in this way are unhealthy. I know that was the case for me. Rarely were there celebrations, family moments, and bonding around healthier food options. I mean no one was saying, "Yes, Auntie Jo got a new job! Let's have baked chicken and broccoli!" Instead, we would celebrate with the most delicious, carb-rich, fat-rich, and sugar-loaded foods we had! As a result, I picked up some not so good habits with food, which lead to being overweight from grade school years until I was about 23 years old. When I got to college, my relationship with food and my personal, romantic relationships seemed to be mirroring each other – no stability, no commitments, taking risks, blurred boundaries, and just "having a good time." Food made me feel good, and I sought out people and situations that did the same. I didn't yet have, at this time, a sense of my self-worth and boundaries, so I sought validation from others and defined my self-worth by the good times I was having with the people around me. And, those good times often involved food!

Food was powerful! It controlled my mood and emotions. It served as both an external source of validation and the glue that held many of my relationships and good times together. Fast forward to my weight loss journey that started in 2004 and training as a psychologist that began in 2008. It wasn't until these times that I started gaining insight into my patterns in relationships and started to understand just how deep my toxic relationship with food ran.

I've been blessed to have battled through my own weight loss journey and to have had training experiences that helped me gain insight into the toxic relationships I had with food. This insight also helped me to understand toxic relationships I had with people. My journey has brought me opportunities where I have been able to learn about myself and work through some of those issues that kept me in a cycle of poor decision-making, poor boundaries, and poor discipline as it related to food and people. Using the same strategies and thought-provoking tips that I'll teach you, I have built a more stable, disciplined, boundary-rich, healthy, and fulfilling relationship with food and people! I still enjoy my good times, and good food, don't get me wrong! The difference now is that food doesn't get the last say so. I do!

"Don't judge me by where I've been. Judge me by where I'm going."

- Dr. Ebony

Introduction

A lot of times on the weight loss journey, we don't get the results that we want. Who am I kidding? *Most* of the time we don't get the results we want. More often than not, it is because our expectations do not match up with our realities – I'll talk more about this later. But, for the most part, I've learned that weight loss results don't happen mainly because we do not recognize that something more profound is at play. Because we don't recognize it, we can't address it.

Getting and maintaining results is so much more than following a meal plan and setting your timer to eat breakfast. Although these factors are helpful to the weight loss process, the actual relationship with food is often completely neglected, especially when there are expectations for quick fixes. We don't realize that to get the lasting results that we want and permanently change how we interact with food, we've got to change the relationship we've built with it. Think about it this way – you wouldn't expect to be completely over your husband/wife or long-term boyfriend/girlfriend in 21 days, right? The same goes for your relationship with food. It takes time to work through the emotional baggage left by that person and situation – the scars, the memories, the good times, the bad times – and, the same goes for the relationships you've built with food. It takes time to work through those emotional hang-ups, memories, negative thoughts, and triggers. It takes even more time to break a lifetime of bad habits. So, if you've ever wondered why you can't seem to get or maintain results from a 21-Day, 30-Day, or 60-Day diet plan – this is why! You haven't tackled the issues at the core. You haven't dealt with your actual relationship with food that you've built over time. The lifetime of bad habits, toxic thoughts, negative emotions, and unrealistic expectations are not, and have not, been addressed.

Throughout this book, I'm going to teach you some ways to get out of those toxic relationships with food and break those unhealthy patterns that have kept you stuck. I am a little old fashioned in that I believe in doing your work, taking your time on your journey, and trusting the process! I don't push or promote quick fixes, and this book is no different. My focus is on helping you build a better relationship with food – that takes time and practice. However, once you break those bad habits and strong holds, you are going to be amazed at your new life! And, believe it or not, you can also use this book to end those toxic and ineffective personal relationships (strong holds) with people as well.

The Courtship

Chapter 1

the start of the relationship

Relationships are everywhere and with everything. You were conceived from a relationship – whether it was romantic or casual. Even before you are born, you start to build relationships with the world around you and throughout your development. You build relationships with your parents' voices, siblings' voices, sounds, etc. As you grow outside of the womb, you start to build even stronger relationships with these people and things. I'm not saying all of these relationships are great, but they're relationships nonetheless. As you develop and grow, you are taught from those around you, and even from your own experiences, how to show up and how to act in relationships. You are even learning what to say to others. You can either pick up some good, healthy habits or you can pick up some poor, toxic habits. The same is true goes for personal relationships as well as relationships you build with food. Just take a minute and think about the things you do or say that you picked up from your mom, dad, aunties, uncles, cousins, and grandparents. So many of these people's habits were passed down to us without us even knowing it, including their habits with food. Too, as we continue to grow and navigate through life, we pick up habits from others and the world around us. These patterns can either be effective or ineffective.

The Company You Keep

Let's use my sister's life experience as an example. Once in a class we were teaching, she talked about her relationship with a co-worker with whom who she had become good friends. They had been hanging out so long that her friend's ways became her ways and my sister's ways became her friend's ways. That's normal for friendships and relationships. What happened to my sister, however, was that she didn't expect to pick up the eating habits that she did from her friend. My sister told the story of when she was at her largest size – she and her friend would each eat three burgers during one sitting. However, she never consumed that much food during one sitting around our family or me. It's not to say that she didn't eat like that alone, though. But, her relationship and pattern of interacting with food were intensified based on the company she was with – based on the relationships present with both her friend and the food. Now, it is likely that she felt more comfortable eating this way with her friend. It could also be the case that ordering and eating this way was almost an automatic response given the history she already had with food. Either way, this is a realistic example of how we build habits and patterns based on our environment and whom we are around. It is also an example of how bad habits and relationships are strengthened and reinforced by elements in your environment that support the bad habits and relationships.

After going through her break-up with toxic food and learning to eat healthier and interact more effectively with food (and people), my sister realized something about her past behavior. She realized that because of the company she kept, her environment, and lack of boundaries and discipline, she picked up specific behavioral patterns from human-to-human relationships that led to the eventual toxic relationships she had formed with food. I love hearing my sister tell this story because it is more evidence that the weight loss journey must take a look at more factors than quick results. If you never address the root issues such as being triggered by old friends and familiar patterns and situations, you might continue to be frustrated that "nothing is working" no matter what you try.

Falling In & Out of Love

Let's take a look at romantic relationships where the same thing sometimes happens. At the beginning of relationships, like in the dating phase, you might find yourself falling in love. When this happens, you want to be around that person all the time, and for many people, a lot of interactions and bonding occurs over food (i.e., dinner, chocolate, drinks, etc.). Or, let's take the ending of a relationship – you might turn to food for comfort, especially if you learned over the course of your life to use food for comfort and companionship. No matter the scenario, in both of these situations, before you know it, you look up, and you've gained 15 pounds (or more)! When you use food for comfort and to cope with loneliness, belonging, sadness, and negative emotions in general, you strengthen that relationship with food. Food doesn't betray you, food is reliable, and you know that food makes you feel good. That kind of bond is very hard to break. Hence, the reason so many people struggle with taking off the pounds! Ending a relationship is already hard, but giving up the food that has been there when no one else has, is even harder! Without addressing this area of difficulty and very real possibility, losing weight and sticking to a plan might be doomed before it starts.

Childhood Trauma & Abuse

Another area where toxic relationships with food forms is through experiences of trauma. A lot of people don't like to talk about this, but it's a common occurrence. In my practice as a psychologist, I've heard stories where people who have been abused and neglected as children or have been in relationships where they experienced domestic violence, verbal abuse, and mental and emotional abuse have used food as an escape or form of protection. Many times women have told me that they have eaten to put on weight without consciously knowing it but somehow figured out that putting on weight protected them. It kept them invisible so they couldn't be seen. If they can't be seen, then they can't be hurt. It kept them in the background so that they didn't stand out. If they didn't stand out, no one would notice they were there to hurt them. In essence, the relationship built with food comforted them. It protected them. So, if something has been your protector all of these years imagine how hard it is to break up with something that has been there to protect you, hide you, comfort you, and keep you safe for so long! That's deep and powerful! And, that type of relationship with food is probably the hardest to undo. But, the good news is that it's hard, NOT IMPOSSIBLE!

Chronic Pain

Being injured or suffering from chronic pain is another source for the development of toxic relationships with food. Sometimes it's easy to turn to food for comfort, especially if you have been injured and are not able to move around as you used to. In a world that has become unfamiliar because you can't navigate it like you used to, food is the "familiar face." Food is the commonplace where you can retreat and feel like yourself again. It's sometimes a feeling of nostalgia. Food has a way of making old memories feel brand new. And, for people who feel like they've been robbed of their lives through injury, illness, or pain, food is stable and consistent and something that doesn't change when everything else around you has changed. That's comforting! And, because of that, it's easy to form toxic relationships with food when looking for that feel good feeling to escape pain and despair. For some clients with chronic pain, learning new ways to eat and interact with food can be very difficult. Because food might be the only way a person feels good and has some relief, he/she might be unwilling to give that up. Also, when food is the only sense of "peace" in your life, it can be difficult to enter the change process, break old habits, and start to learn new habits.

A Real Life Example

Let's look at an example of a client, Sheila[1], who experienced an unfortunate car accident and continuously suffered from back and knee pain. As she recovered from her injuries, she started eating a lot of foods that were unhealthy. Although unhealthy, the food comforted her while she was recovering and she built a relationship where she counted on food to feel better and to feel comforted. Now, Sheila has recovered from her injuries, and her knee pain has improved. However, she gained 30 lbs. while doing so and is finding it hard to lose the weight and break the bad habits she built with food. Her narrative has been that she can't lose weight because of her injuries. After several unsuccessful attempts at losing weight and feeling frustrated with diets and meal plans, Shelia decided to stop trying to lose weight and just live with her life like it was, even though she was not happy about it. But, after our work together, she started to realize and accept that her reliance on food for comfort was the primary reason she had not been successful in her weight loss endeavors. During her injury recovery, Sheila learned to use food to improve her mood; thus her toxic relationship with food grew stronger. Now, she was scared that breaking up with food would leave her without anyone or anything to help her when she was feeling down. After some time together, she began to work through negative thoughts, fear, and habits that were keeping her stuck.

---

[1] Client's name changed to protect confidentiality.

Although she continues to struggle from time to time to break the bad habits and relationship with food, her weight loss process has been more consistent than it ever has been. She has learned new ways to cope without food, and regularly practices disrupting the toxic relationship she had with food.

Sadly, many women, and men, have stories like Sheila. Their toxic relationship with food is so strong that they can't seem to break away from it. It becomes so hard and frustrating that they give up and sink back down into the comfortable and familiar place, even if it's unhealthy for them. But, that stops NOW! As I did with Sheila, I'm going to help you get out of that rut and get your life back!

"Always have a plan for how to make yourself better. Period.

- Dr. Ebony

Making the Relationship Official

Chapter 2

creating and maintaining your narrative

Throughout my practice as a psychologist and health coach, when it's time to talk about implementing change, I've heard several of my clients say, "Well, I take medication. I have five doses of this, six doses of that. I have inflammation. I take steroids. I have all these things going on. I can't lose weight. Nothing works." Others have also said, "I have a bad back. I had knee surgery. I can't go to the gym? I can't work out, and that's why I can't lose weight." Many of these issues are very real and present a big hindrance to the weight loss process. That's not a question. However, regardless of the real-life situation and narrative, my next questions are, "What are you eating? Do you have to eat the six Oreo's before bed? How does that help with the pain? Do you have to eat a second helping of gumbo?" What does that do for the inflammation? Do you need that other basket of bread at the restaurant?" How is that helping the steroids? Do you need the sweets and chips? What do they do for the back pain?" The response is always a resounding, "I hadn't thought about it like that until you said something."

The narratives that we have created have become our personal stories and go-to explanations for parts of our lives where we feel like we have no control. Also, the justifications and excuses help us to feel better about why we haven't accomplished that health or weight loss goal. Furthermore, it is rare that people realize that their narrative is the very thing making it more difficult to lose weight and end the unhealthy relationships with food.

Part of the process in disrupting these sorts of narratives is by identifying reality for what it is. When I hear clients start in with similar narratives, I let them know that, "Yes, it has been difficult. But, let's look at some other reasons why losing weight has been so hard for you. Let's consider a few things." After all, if you never take each puzzle piece into consideration, it'll be really difficult to create a full, finished picture.

After it has become clear that the familiar narrative is helping to maintain a toxic relationship with food, we begin to do real work in reality. Specific patterns and things you do on a daily basis help to maintain your narrative. However, disrupting aspects of your real life and behavior helps to create shifts in those narratives and changes them from ineffective to effective. One of the ways we can do this is by starting in the kitchen – which is the primary factor in the weight gain/weight loss reality. For instance, consider how you might answer the following, "What is in your kitchen that is not helping with the pain, the medicines, the inflammation, the high blood pressure, thyroid issues, etc.? What might be causing each of these issues to become worse?" You might point out sodas, cookies, bread, desserts, alcohol, etc. Helping you to physically see things about your environment that aren't helping you reach your goals is powerful because it takes what you once thought was impossible to change and makes it possible. Moreover, you might realize that you can make better choices about what you bring into your home to eat. As a result, you start to feel powerful over your circumstances and more capable of making different decisions that will help you reach your goals! It is no longer something that is out of your control.

Once you make those changes in your reality, your old narrative starts to shift and crumble. Now, you're making room for a new narrative that pushes you towards your goals instead of away from them. The development of a new narrative might sound like this, "Yes, I have back pain. And, yes, I just had knee surgery. Although it is difficult for me to go to the gym and work out, I am making better choices with how I am eating. I make more conscious decisions to bring food into my home that helps me reach my goals." Now, doesn't that sound empowering? With this type of narrative, you are speaking a different reality into existence. You are creating a space for different, more efficient, and healthier behaviors to develop.

A lot of times your relationship with food will lie to you and lead you to a narrative that justifies that relationship staying around. It's no different than being in an abusive relationship that you just can't see to leave. In an abusive relationship, the abuser will start to make you believe that the abuse is your fault and that there is nothing you can do to change the situation. And, if you leave, you're going to be miserable. The abuser leads you to believe that people are wrong and that people are against you.

You might even be made to think that no one wants anything good for you and that you will never be anything in life. When you're in an abusive relationship, the abuser breaks you down so that they can have control over you. So basically, you start to feel powerless, like you don't have a way out, and will just have to deal with it. Does that sound OK? Of course not! But, the same type of thing is happening all the time when we justify our eating behaviors!

A toxic relationship with food will start to make you believe that no one will ever be able to help you and there is no way anyone can help you get out of this place. You might even start to justify your reality by saying, "You know what, it's not that bad. I'm really okay. It's just food. It's not going to kill me." In the same way the abused person starts to feel in an abusive relationship, our narratives about why we can't lose weight (for whatever reason) and why it'll never happen for us, also leaves us feeling powerless, out of control, and like we just have to deal with it. But, that is a lie! You can do something about it. You can change your situation. You can regain control. Your narrative can be different.

The only difference between a toxic relationship with food and being in a relationship with someone who is physically abusive is the amount of control we have in the relationship. We can control food and the way in which we interact with different foods. And, although we do have the ability to control our choices about the type of people we get into relationships with, we cannot control the other person's behavior. Since we have more ability to control ourselves and our actions, we can change those behaviors and narratives that are not working for us. Once your narrative changes, the things around you start to change and how you navigate the world changes as well. And, before you know it, you are a healthier version of yourself – both mentally and physically!

"You would tell your friend, 'Girl, you deserve better' if she was in a relationship with someone beating on her. But, how many times have you told her, 'Girl, you deserve better' when you saw her eating food you knew was killing her?"

- Dr. Ebony

Catching Feelings

Chapter 3

what do emotions have to do with it?

Changing your narrative and changing the way you speak about yourself is great! However, getting there can be a difficult task because that narrative is usually deeply etched in your mind and emotions. Once emotions sink their teeth into a situation, they don't want to let go! Narratives that are profoundly rooted in feelings, as most are, can become so automatic that you don't readily recognize them as excuses or justifications. Instead, your narrative starts to sound like cold, hard facts. And, we all know how hard it is to argue with facts, even those we've made up in our minds.

Emotions have the ability to dictate our behaviors and experiences. Emotions also impact our thoughts…and, vice versa. Since our narratives are essentially thoughts, beliefs, and ideas, they influence our behaviors and experiences just as our actions and experiences impact our narratives. Therefore, if you've come to adopt a particular narrative, no matter what it is, chances are, you have some powerful emotions around that narrative and what it means for you. Breaking away from those feelings is just as important as breaking away from that narrative. It's not easy to do away with a narrative that makes you feel justified in your choices, even if the decisions are not useful for you. For instance, the person who says that they cannot lose weight because of steroids and knee pain might feel a lot less guilty about the weight that they've gained. Their narrative about medicine and pain lessens their emotional experience of guilt, while at the same time minimizing the impact that their ineffective behaviors such as overeating, poor food choices, lack of sleep, etc. might have had on gaining weight. Because the cycle of guilt can feel so overwhelming and create more overeating and poor food choices, it's more comfortable to hold on to the medicine and pain narrative as facts rather than deal with the guilt of their own behavior.

Toxic relationships with food are formed and maintained in this way. The narrative keeps us from feeling sad, guilty, and wrong about where we stand on our goals. In turn, we don't have to do much about changing our current situation because we learn to rely on the narrative to justify and make sense of our current situation (i.e., weight gain). There's no real responsibility for your own actions and behaviors, and blame is placed on external factors. When this happens, we permit ourselves to engage in the same ineffective patterns with food that causes us to gain weight, feel bad, and become unhealthy. You see, the cycle remains true. Your thoughts (narrative) impact your emotions (less guilt), and your emotions (less guilt) affect your behaviors (continuing to make poor food choices). This type of cycle is the root of many toxic relationships with food.

On another token, toxic relationships with food can involve a different interaction of emotions, thoughts, and behaviors. Using food to soothe and release negative emotional experiences can be a difficult situation to resolve as well. Typically referred to as emotional eating, the cycle involves feeling an emotion (commonly a negative emotion such as loneliness), then engaging in a behavior to reduce that emotion (eating carb-rich, fatty, processed foods) and, in turn, not feeling as lonely anymore (temporary relief from intense loneliness). The cycle of emotional eating is strengthened and challenging to interrupt because the immediate relief from the negative emotion, although brief, can feel much more beneficial than the long-term cost of the behavior (weight gain, health issues, etc.). Many times, the benefit of happiness from food is so great, that regardless of the consequence to the physical body, you might not be willing to let go of that relationship/cycle, especially when you have not learned other ways of coping to deal with such intense emotions.

These types of cycles involving emotions let us know that the emotional experience is very significant in the weight loss process. Any diet plan, program, or training regimen that does not include emotional work is neglecting to address a vast part of the root problem for many people. The reason that you might not have been able to stick to a particular plan or routine and why you often feel like that nothing works might be because the relationship with food at the emotional level has not been addressed. The emotional experience, in essence, is the glue that keeps relationships together as well as the thorn that makes it difficult to recover from painful relationships. Consider your most successful personal relationship. Now, consider the relationship that makes you grit your teeth and roll your eyes every time you think about it. Regardless of the outcome of the relationship, there was a deep emotional attachment, be it love or hate. Whether progressing a relationship to the next level or getting over the hurt of the most painful relationship, both situations require that you do some work at the emotional level. The same is true for relationships with food. Whether you're building a healthy relationship with food or healing from a toxic relationship with food, you have to do deal with your emotions and approach your interaction with food from a healthier emotional place.

Trouble in Paradise

Chapter 4

when emotions cut deep

For people who struggle with intense, negative emotional issues, including depression and anxiety, it can be challenging to get out of those emotional states. And, it is sometimes easier to cope and soothe oneself by turning to food. Remember, from the time we come into this world eating is paired with emotional experiences and food is the go-to for reducing unwanted emotions. So, as we navigate the world and try to figure out how to cope with intense, negative emotions, eating becomes the way we learn to reduce, suppress, and distract from emotions we don't want to feel, especially in the absence of other adequate and fast-acting coping skills. Hence, creating the foundation for a toxic relationship with food.

Emotional states like depression and anxiety can also be deeply rooted in painful pasts so much so that addressing on the issue(s) that caused the depression or anxiety can be too overwhelming. It might be too painful to address the root issue and try to lose weight at the same time. So, some people might go with the lesser of the two evils and attempt to work on the weight issue and "deal with all that other stuff later." However, it is unrealistic to think that the more profound problems don't have to be addressed as well. Because, the truth is, if you work on the weight issue and do lose weight and end up with a slimmer body, the root problems that created the depression and anxiety are still there. In fact, what you have now is a smaller physical body with the same mental anguish, emotional hang-ups, and negative thoughts that continue to bother you just as before. Thus, keeping a space open for those same ineffective coping skills such as overeating, late night snacking, not eating, and other poor food choices to creep back into your life.

As much as you attempt to distract from the work that must be done, sooner or later, you will have to clear up the infection at the root. Or, it will continue to spread illness and disease throughout every part of your life until you have no choice but to address it. When the infection spreads, even the healthiest parts of the body are infected. Moreover, if you carry negative thoughts and beliefs into your physically slimmer body, those same negative thoughts and ideas have a high chance of continuing to affect your self-esteem how you see yourself, no matter how small, or skinny, you become. Negative thoughts and emotions might lead you to be very critical and judgmental of yourself and judge your progress as not good enough or you might continue to nitpick at everything on your body and tell yourself that you still need to do more. Deeper emotional issues, although difficult, if they aren't addressed will discredit your success, progress, and efforts every time! It's hard to end a toxic relationship with food (or anything for that matter) when all you keep telling yourself is that you're not doing enough or that you're still not good enough.

Some experiences like those associated with betrayal, rejection, bullying, neglect, trauma, and even death can run a bit deeper than others. In situations such as these, food can easily become the replacement for a companion, friend, and confidant when you feel that you cannot count on actual people to serve in these roles. Also, because these types of experiences hurt so badly and can sometimes rattle you at your core, you might feel vulnerable, and safer, turning to food instead. In fact, the reliance on food for coping in the presence of emotions that don't feel good might be an automatic response, especially if that's been your go-to way of coping since childhood.

If you feel like I'm talking directly to you and like I'm all up in your business, well that's because I am! But, what I want you to remember is that what's happening to you is common and ordinary. Many of you were born into this way of coping because those around you also coped in this way. However, because it's familiar and routine, that doesn't mean that you still can't do something about those behaviors and relationships with food that are causing problems for you. You absolutely can! You can change your relationship with food regardless of what emotion is present. Learning more effective coping skills that do not necessarily involve food will give you a head start on actually getting the results you want when embarking on your weight loss journey. After reading this book, I am hopeful that you will continue to reshape your narrative from one that leaves you powerless to one that leaves you empowered and encouraged!

"Don't judge me for where I've been. Judge me by where I'm going."

- Dr. Ebony

The Breakup
Breaking up for good

Chapter 5

acknowledge that you're in a toxic relationship

Hello. My name is (go ahead, say your name) and I have a toxic relationship with food.

Great! That was the first step!

Ok, it might not be that easy. But, the first thing you have to do to end your toxic relationship with food is acknowledge that you are actually in an unhealthy relationship. Just like in an unhealthy relationship with someone you know is cheating on you, you cannot move forward until you acknowledge that the cheating is happening. You cannot move beyond that situation until you recognize that you are in the unhealthy relationship. Failure to acknowledge the toxic relationship while minimizing and justifying it might suggest that you're in denial about the state of the relationship. And, as long as you live in a state of denial about your toxic relationships, you'll never be able to break up, move on, and heal.

Let's be real; you've heard it before. You've heard your girlfriends or someone you know minimize or justify their unhealthy relationship with someone. An example of minimizing might sound like, "He pushed me, but he didn't hit me." Or, "He hit me, but girl, it didn't leave a mark like what 'John' did to 'Mary.' It wasn't that bad." On the other hand, justification might sound like, "Yeah, he cheated, but I'm never home, and a man has needs." Or, "My mouth is smart. Sometimes I push him too far."

Wait! Before you close the book and start cursing at the statements above, you might say many of those same statements concerning your own unhealthy relationships with food. The difference is, the justification and minimization might not be so easy to recognize. But, don't worry. I'm going to help you out.

Sometimes when things are too hard for us to face or change, we try to lessen the severity of it so that it's easier to deal with. That's called minimizing. Other times, when the reality is too hard of a pill to swallow, and we are resistant to our reality, we try to change the reality by making excuses for why something is happening so that we are okay with it. That's called justifying. The same thing happens with food.

Denial about your current situation with food and just how bad it is can show up in many ways. Sometimes you don't even have to verbally admit that you're in denial for you to be living in a constant state of denial. For instance, the fact that you pride yourself on being able to wear those stretchy tights and flowy shirt still although you've gained 20 lbs., is a form of denial. If you were to put words to that experience, it might sound like, "Well, I must not have gained that much weight. I can still wear my favorite tights and shirt." Of course, you can! The pants are stretch material and the shirt is naturally loose fitting. As long as you can justify (lie) to yourself that because you can still wear your clothes, then the problem must not be that bad, then you are setting yourself up to live in a state of denial. However, this might be okay with you. The good news is that when you live in a state of denial, you never have to do anything about the "problem," which leaves you unaccountable. However, the downside to that is that you know the real truth regardless of what others can see or what you can cover up. You know that the problem isn't going anywhere and sooner or later, you will have to face it.

Some more examples of being in denial (just in case that one didn't hit home) that we see often is through social media. Social media makes it very easy to be in denial, with yourself and with the public, about your issues with food and your weight. You can take a picture just right to get the angle that makes you look the slimmest. You can crop yourself out of images. You can take a million selfies where no one has to see your full body. All of these tactics are great for those not so good outfit days or days where you're feeling more bloated than usual. However, using social media to intentionally send false messages about how you actually look and feel, without any intention of working on your problems, only leaves you feeling worse about yourself in the end. After all, once you post the picture and the likes and shares rake in, you're still left with how you feel about yourself deep down. No angle on a camera, filter, or editing software can ever do the work that you need to do to end your toxic relationship with food, honestly. Avoiding the root issues and failing to acknowledge that your problem might be more significant than you thought, leaves you in a sunken place of denial.

Let's look at a few more examples of what denial might sound like in narrative form. One that I actually used to say or have heard so many times is, "I'm just big boned. My family is big boned." Or, another good one, "I just am carrying a lot of water weight." And, finally, "This is baby weight." Whether true at some point or not, all of these phrases have been used to justify and minimize the real work that needs to be done to reach weight loss goals. When you say that you're "big boned," what you're essentially saying is that no matter what you do, you'll always be of a certain size and build. Well, that's sort of true and very false, at the same time. While not everyone is meant to be skinny or small, if there is excess fat and weight that needs to lose your body, changing your eating and activity habits will make that happen. When you truly clean up your diet and change your lifestyle, you cannot control where you lose weight on your body. However, by relying on the "I'm just big boned" justification, many times this leaves room for you to not go all in or not be 100% accountable like you need to be in order to reach your goals. This type of justification lets you do just enough to get by.

With regard to the water weight, sometimes there are legit reasons as to why water retention is a problem for many people, such as medical issues or medication. However, more times than not, water retention is an issue related to the types of food being eaten. By passing weight gain off as simply water retention from medical issues or medication, you never have to take a real look at the foods that you're eating. That's minimizing and, ultimately, denial, especially, if you know you're not eating healthy a majority of the time – and, you know this truth regardless of what you tell others.

Lastly, let's address the baby weight narrative. First, if you are a mother, congratulations! My hat goes off to you! Now, if you are a mother who is still using the baby weight justification a year or years after the baby is born, then we might have some issues with denial. Yes, it is more difficult to get weight off after a baby. But, it's not impossible! It's more difficult to get weight off after having a baby if your eating habits have not changed to what they need to be in order to shed weight. Ordering a dessert after every meal and eating second servings of meals is not a function of "baby weight." Instead, that's a function of over eating, a lack of discipline, and a lack of appropriate boundaries…also known as a toxic relationship with food. However, what some women do after they've had children is blame their weight gain or inability to lose weight on having a baby. As previously stated, yes, it can be more difficult, but realistically, the baby cannot always take responsibility for your choices!

No, I don't have children and I have never been pregnant (in case you're reading this and becoming upset with me), but I have been someone who has hidden behind excuses before when I didn't want to or didn't know how to do the work. At times when I honestly thought it was impossible for me to lose weight, my narrative was filled with phrases that justified or minimized my food behaviors. You don't have to be a mother or have ever been pregnant to understand this concept. Anyone with a busy schedule or trying to tackle life after a major life event will struggle to find time to do what they need to do to create a healthier lifestyle. That's not just relative to mothers. And, because the struggle is not specific to one particular group, the good news is that with some real acknowledgement of the problem(s), diligence in changing the problem, and accountability, anybody can turn their situation around and create a healthier relationship with food! When you don't exclude yourself and limit your possibilities, you begin to feel powerful over your situation and empowered to take responsibility and control over what has been keeping you stuck!

Although it is easier to be in denial and not acknowledge the consequences of your toxic relationship with food, this doesn't make the problem go away. The relationship and poor food choices are still there. You can ignore a black eye and wear shades and all of the Fenty concealer at Sephora, but the truth is that the black eye is still there. It still happened. Denial pushes away your responsibility for changing your situation and, in the end, leaves you feeling powerless. When you're powerless, you cannot change your situation and recover. But, when you stand up and change your narrative to, "Yes, this is happening to me. It's hard. And, I can still make some changes and turn things around for myself", you regain the control that was lost and recovery can begin!

Chapter 6

unfold your arms and open your mind

In order to *do* something different, you first have to make it up in your mind that you are going to do it. Everything that you do starts with a thought, even before the action is ever carried out. For example, ordering cheese nachos instead of a chicken sandwich happens as a thought first. The thoughts occur so fast that you might not notice it all the time. Nevertheless, the thoughts are there first. Thus, before changing your behaviors (i.e., overeating, late night snacking, buying groceries, not eating, etc.), you have to change your thoughts first. Changing your thoughts and your old ways of thinking is how you change your mindset, and eventually, those old habits that keep you stuck and frustrated. But, you can't walk into a new mindset and new way of interacting with food, with your arms folded and full of skepticism and criticism.

One of the questions that I get most often when I talk to my clients about changing their mindsets is, "How do I actually do that?" Changing your mindset and relationship with food requires that you have an openness, and willingness, to learning and doing something different. It is not the time for your stubbornness and pride to get in the way, although that is what usually happens when you're trying to change. Your stubbornness is fertile ground for skepticism and criticism. It doesn't allow you to move beyond your comfort zone and it keeps you stuck.

As humans, we become so accustomed to the same way of doing things and carrying out our lives that when something changes, it can make us feel off-kilter and out of control. Most of you can probably tell me what you have planned for two weeks and one day from now. That's just how much we operate out of automation, routine, and habit. Keeping a schedule and planning your life out is not bad! It might only become a problem when you leave no room in your life for flexibility and new habits that will help you function better, which is the case for most people who are stuck, stubborn, and stressed. We can become so loyal to our scheduled lives that even if it's chaotic, stressful, and causing us to become ill, we will keep on living the same way because "it's what we know." We learn to operate in our own chaos and something new is scary and makes us feel out of control. Yes, it can be scary to change, yet the fact remains that if you are going to change your weight and poor food choices, your mindset has to change as well; you have to be open to operating in a different way.

Changing your mindset means that sometimes you are going to have to be okay with being WRONG! You are going to have to be okay with learning that not everything you thought or learned is true. Accepting this part of the change process helps you to gradually let go of the old teachings that have been passed down to you and that you've carried around with you for so long. Remember, this will take some time! At times it might seem like you're going against everything you thought you knew, and that's because you are! But, let's look at the bright side – your old ways of thinking and behaving are the very things that have kept you stuck anyway. And, has that worked for you? Chances are it has not.

Changing the ways that you think is one of the most laborious processes in the weight loss and health journey! In fact, losing weight is primarily a mental battle where you're fighting to change the way you think about food, your weight, and your eating habits that you've had since you were a child, in many cases. This 'ish is hard! Trying to undo 30 years of thoughts and habits is not an overnight feat. So, to think that a 30-day fix will cure all of your weight and food problems is unrealistic. Yet, this is the reason some people can't see weight loss programs to the end and get the results they want. They want the physical change but have been too stubborn and afraid to do the necessary mental work along the way. I understand it - it's common to want a quick fix when you're in a place of desperation. However, changing your mindset does not happen that way. Creating a new mindset requires that you challenge old thoughts over and over and over…and, over again. It's a process you have to be willing to go through if you want to create a lifestyle and relationship with food that's different than you have now.

Ending a toxic relationship with food does not happen with skepticism and criticism being your automatic response. In case you don't understand what skepticism and criticism sound like, let's look at some examples. Upon learning that you aren't eating enough, you respond with, "Oh, I can't eat that much. That's not going to work for me. That's not for people like me", chances are you're skeptical and you have your arms folded to the process. Or, if you have the thought, "That program will never work for me. It doesn't have the foods I love built into the program and that's not going to work", your criticism could be blocking your progress.

When you apply these same concepts to a romantic relationship, the process is very similar. If there is someone you know wants to leave a relationship where there is domestic violence, they have to make up in their mind that they want to leave before they actually choose to leave. Nothing you say will make a difference unless that person has made up in their mind that they are ready to do something different. In the same ways as the weight loss process, fear, frustration, and desperation will be present for that person. Skepticism and criticism will likely be present as well. However, if the person is going to change their situation eventually, they will need to work through the skepticism and criticism that keeps them stuck in order to improve their mindset to be willing to even explore their options for leaving.

Overall, an essential step in ending your toxic relationship with food is realizing that your mindset will need to change and that IT TAKES TIME! (Cue the startup of a chapter on patience…not really! That would be a whole different book).

"There will never be a right time to get started. There will always be something going on! Stop making excuses."

- Dr. Ebony

"Trust your process."

- Dr. Ebony

Chapter 7

it's not black & white

If you've ever gone on a diet or tried to lose weight, then you know the process is way more complicated than it sometimes seems. While on the one hand the concepts of dieting can be simple, actually creating a new lifestyle can be quite complicated. The process is not black and white. Yet you, like me and so many others, might have been guilty a time or two of embarking on your weight loss journey with black and white thinking, then, asking yourself why "nothing works."

To break up with food and end that toxic relationship, you're going to have to give up your stubborn ways of thinking, or nothing will ever seem like it works for you. Believe it or not, there is space for several different methods of living healthier to exist at one time. Specifically, when you're adopting a healthier lifestyle, IT DOES NOT MEAN THAT YOU CAN'T HAVE FOODS YOU LIKE AND LOVE. That's actually not the case at all. Having a healthy lifestyle means that you can eat healthier AND you can enjoy the foods you love. Both of these things can exist together, with balance of course. Once you understand that, your task would then be to figure out how to organize the times at which you eat healthier foods and times when you eat the other foods that you love. Instead of worrying about what you can't eat, which is mostly rooted in black and white thinking, start building a healthier relationship with food by understanding balance, frequency, and timing of food in your diet.

Trying to Achieve Perfection

The first step people commonly take when they start new diets and ways of eating is to become eerily restrictive. Usually when you're trying to achieve perfection in your new diet program, this is because anxiety, worry, confusion, and misunderstanding is filling your mind. Black and white thinking will lead you to believe that if you don't follow a program to the letter that you won't lose the weight. This isn't true. Adhering to a plan with about an 80% accuracy and consistency will yield results. Although it comes from a good place, trying to achieve perfection through strict adherence to any diet is a recipe for rebellion and relapse. Think about when you were a teenager, being told not to do something usually ended up with you doing it anyway. But, the more flexibility you had, the more responsible you were in your choices. Your relationship with food is the same way! Placing too many restrictions on yourself leaves you feeling boxed in and without options. When you feel like you have no choices in the program, you will rebel.

It is also when you have no self-control that you become incredibly restrictive and allow black and white (either/or) type thinking to rule your attempts at creating change. For example, you might believe that for you to avoid overeating, you don't need to eat at all. This type of thinking doesn't work and increases your chances of binge eating. It also shortens the lifespan of your diet. You will become frustrated quickly and return to your old ways of eating in no time if this is the way you approach losing weight.

Relying on the Scale to See Results

The most common example of black and white thinking is related to the overuse of the scale and subsequent thoughts that the scale is the most essential part of the weight loss journey. If you feel that the scale is the only way that you can tell if you are achieving results or not, chances are you are engaging in black and white thinking. Along the same lines, if you believe that you aren't doing enough, or aren't good enough because the scale doesn't show what you want it to show, chances are you are engaging in black and white thinking. Even though most of us have been brainwashed to believe that the scale is the end all be all, it really is just a small component of the weight loss process. And, relying only on the scale for your validation that you're on the right track and doing well or that what you're doing is working, is a set up for disaster. Talk about feeling like a failure! This type of interaction with the scale can leave you feeling intense negative emotions like disappointment, sadness, and guilt, which can send you into a cycle of emotional eating, rebellion, and relapse-like we discussed in Chapter 3.

Restricting to Certain Types of Programs or Foods

Black and white thinking also shows up in the types of diets you choose. If black and white thinking has ever controlled your choices, it is likely because you haven't learned that other options are available. For instance, I've heard countless people say that the only way they can lose weight is if they drink juices or smoothies, stop eating meat, or stop eating bread. These types of restrictions typically come from a place of miseducation about what it really takes to lose weight. When people feel like they don't know what to expect, it feels safer to stick with what you know, even if what you know is false. That's why so many people, no matter how many times it didn't work for them in the past, will continue to restrict bread and meat when trying to lose weight no matter the evidence that shows that you can lose weight while eating bread and meat. Sometimes that's all they believe will work in the weight loss process. And, in their minds, they've been taught that less food (more restriction) is how you lose weight. The black and white thinking will not allow them to think beyond what they "know" to try something different.

Sometimes a common thought is that you have to only eat bell peppers and carrots in order for you to be healthy. And, that you can't possibly eat pizza and wings and be healthy. Neither way of thinking promotes a healthy relationship with food. That's why that type of thinking stops now! I want to introduce you to a new way of looking at your weight loss and health journey. I want to help you see that two things can happen at the same time. You can be healthy AND eat pizza and wings…with balance! Seeing it from this perspective helps to loosen up the black and white thinking and invites some flexibility into your lifestyle. With flexibility comes the freedom of choice and control! When you feel more in control, you feel more powerful and confident about your abilities to change.

"Sometimes it's not the physical weight that's the problem. It's the emotional weight that nobody can see that is the heaviest."

- Dr. Ebony

Chapter 8

if you can't trust YOU, who can you trust?

Trust is not a word you hear often enough in the weight loss process. We need to have more conversations about trust more frequently because there's a certain level of trust you have to have with the weight loss process itself. Even more importantly, you have to establish trust with yourself as well as those around you helping you to reach your goals. Trust is a necessary component in the process of such significant change and quite necessary when embarking on a journey into the unknown. Changing your relationship with food and losing weight is not an easy process and many times the results can be further in the future than you might like. In fact, there's not an immediate return on your investment when you're losing weight and changing your relationship with food. The reward of your hard work is often far removed from the actual work. And, you have to establish trust with the process in order to hold on to the fact that if you keep working, your results will show up.

More than trusting the process or others, you have to learn how to trust yourself when changing your relationship with food. You're the only person who can instill discipline, accountability, and boundaries within your life. Yes, others can guide you on what to do and not do, but you're the only one who can actually DO IT! That's why trusting yourself is so paramount. What you can guide yourself to do when no one is there to hold you accountable will speak to the amount of trust you have in your abilities to create the changes you want to see. Let's face it, the only person who is going to be around you to hold you accountable 24 hours out of the day, every minute of the day, is you. Nobody else can do that. Your mindset is your own, and you're going to have to own the fact that you are the one who has the final say so in what you do. But, if you don't trust yourself enough to hold yourself accountable, changing your relationship with food is going to be much more difficult.

When you don't trust yourself to make choices that will keep you healthy, it is that much more difficult to believe that someone else will be able to guide you to do the same. A lack of trust is where skepticism and being overly critical of your process comes in as well. You might make comments to yourself such as, "I need somebody to be there with me. I don't trust myself to do right on my own." Or, "I'm not going to do right when I go home. I already know me." Also, you might say, "I don't think that what I'm doing is working. I'm not doing enough." When you don't trust yourself and your efforts, you can guarantee that it will always show up in your discipline, motivation, and consistency.

Maybe somewhere in your life up to this point you learned that you couldn't trust yourself. Perhaps your poor decisions in friends, partners, clothes, hairstyles, finances, etc. left you feeling like you don't make the right choices, and therefore, you can't be trusted. Wherever the lack of trust in yourself happened, if you don't process and correct it, you'll always be searching for something or someone to give you what you can't give to yourself. To fully break up with toxic food, you have to be able to trust you to take care of YOU!

Because when food is not there, what will you have? Do you believe you're capable of giving yourself something else? Even if it's control over saying, "No," to food that isn't healthy or helpful, you will have to make those decisions with confidence. It's challenging to be confident in your decisions when you don't trust yourself.

I remember when I was going to therapy during my divorce and my therapist said something to me so profound about my ability to trust myself. She said, "You don't trust you to take care of you, do you?" I was stunned. Because the truth was, I didn't! I didn't trust me to be able to take care of me, and I had given that responsibility to somebody else. In fact, I learned over my life to do that. I didn't have any confidence that I would be okay if I were not in that relationship. Like many of you, that lack of confidence and trust left me reliant on someone else for my security. Hence, when it looked like it was about to be ripped from me, I was resistant and continued to fight for power, control, and I had a huge need to be "right"...because that gave me power too.

You might be having the same struggle in your personal relationships or relationship with food. Your resistance to change could be an indication that you don't completely trust your process or trust that you can be successful in changing. One way to build confidence in yourself is by opening yourself up to having new, different, and sometimes uncomfortable experiences. Being pushed past your comfort zone might be just what you need to break out of those bad habits and learn to trust yourself. When you build trust in yourself, you can walk away from people and things that no longer serve you. When you don't believe in yourself guess what is likely to happen? You guessed it! You stay inside of the toxic relationships you know isn't working. Learning to trust yourself gives you confidence and power to walk away and *know* that you're going to be okay!

"Don't judge me for where I've been. Judge me by where I'm going."

- Dr. Ebony

Chapter 9

birds of a feather…

It's tough to reach the top if you have people at the bottom pulling you back down. You probably know from experience that if you want to reach the top or accomplish any goal, you have to position yourself around people who will help you do so. Negative Nancy's and Skeptical Sara's will be plentiful on your journey. But, when you're breaking up with food or changing any habits, for that matter, it is imperative that you seek out people with similar interests and goals. I can almost guarantee you that at some point throughout your health journey you will have a naysayer or someone voice their opinion about what you're doing and your ability to succeed. Having a clear sense of your goals and a tight network of support will help to keep you grounded as you move towards crushing your goals.

Everybody doesn't belong on this journey with you! I'm not saying that you have to do away with any and everybody who is skeptical. No. That's not what I'm saying. But, what I am a saying is that you won't be able to share your goals with everyone. Not everybody will understand where you're trying to go. And, because they're likely not quite ready to change in their own lives, they may try to talk you out of your goals to keep themselves comfortable. You've got to let these types of people watch your journey from the sidelines.

Positioning yourself around people who are like-minded and have similar goals increases your chances of succeeding. Aligning yourself with people who are also creating a healthier lifestyle and building a healthier relationship with food helps you to create a community that supports you and also keeps you accountable. Growing a healthier relationship with food and changing your habits is a process that requires support because your mind and body will want to quit and run to what's familiar. You need to put people in your corner who will uplift you when you can't uplift yourself. The old saying, "Birds of a feather flock together," is real and applicable to your health journey. Birds fly together because they understand that together they create more resistance against the wind. In the same way, when you have a network of people who support you and are on a similar journey, you are creating more resistance against the old ways of being and the urge to return to those old ways that were keeping you stuck.

Misery loves company

I wish that I could tell you that everybody is going to be happy for you and wish you well on your journey to a healthier lifestyle. But, I can't. I learned the hard way that not everybody is as excited as you are that you're choosing to focus on your health and LIVE! It sounds crazy, doesn't it? I mean, who wouldn't want you to live a longer life without illness, disease, fatigue, and discomfort? The sad reality is that most people will tell you that they want a healthier life for you. But, when you start surpassing them and making them feel guilty for not reaching their own goals, it can get nasty. To be fair to these people, who we will refer to as "the miserables," all of your hard work is a blatant reminder of what they're not doing. That's uncomfortable to watch and hard to accept. Sometimes people will want you to stay where you are because it helps them look better and not feel bad about themselves. Other times, they want you to go back on your promises to yourself because they've gone back on their promises to themselves.

But, there's good news! That's their problem. Not yours! Don't be surprised that as you continue to crush your goals and it shows on your physical body, that "the miserables" will tell you, "Stop losing weight. That's enough." They might even say, "You don't need to lose weight; I like you like this." Again, *their* problem, not yours. In fact, the miserables will be the first to stop inviting you out for dinner because they don't want you to police their food choices. They might also single you out when they "catch" you eating something that they don't think you should be eating. The miserables might have a good heart overall, and they might "say" they support you, but their own lack of discipline and lack of results keeps them in the space of negativity that they try to impose onto others for their personal comfort. The more company they have to live in their misery (and, not work on their goals), the less guilty they feel about where they are. Well, not this year! This year, decline the invite. You don't have to push the miserables all the way out of your life, but their invitation for you to sit with them must be declined. That's why you must start building a community of people who will cheer for you, lift you up, get you back on track, and mean it.

"When food shows you who it is, believe it!"

- Dr. Ebony

"Misery loves company. Decline the invite."

- Dr. Ebony

Chapter 10

be willing to stand alone

I know how it feels to travel your journey alone. There were times when I've had to walk alone as I built a healthier relationship with food. I've also walked apart from others during some of the most challenging transitions in my personal relationships. The ending of my marriage and the shift in my relationship with food were similar processes. Both of them required that, at some point, I rely on none else but myself.

When I left my marriage, I felt utterly alone. I was losing a partner, a best friend, and a family. I didn't recognize it right away, but after going through the process (more like a storm), I realized that I had to be honest with myself about the relationships that were ending. I had to come to terms with whether or not those relationships would help me to live authentically as myself and reach my goals in life. It was scary. It was hard. It was uncomfortable. It felt like all that I knew of my life was ending. Not only was the process and changes uncomfortable for me, but they were also uncomfortable for almost everyone around me.

Some people said, "Oh! I can't believe you're leaving a good man." At the time, this made me feel guilty. However, in hindsight, what I learned about what they were saying was that my relationship felt comfortable and hopeful to them. If I changed that, I would shatter their dreams, hopes, and ideas of a "good man," stable relationship, and successful marriage. Don't get me wrong. There were a few people who I believe honestly thought it was best for me to stay in that relationship for whatever reason. But, for the most part, I think people offered their opinion on what I should do because any changes would mean something different for them and their reality…and, that was uncomfortable.

Looking back, I now recognize that what felt like abandonment at the time was just everyone trying to adjust to changes and all of our new realities. Sometimes when change happens, and people don't know how to react, they might pull away, which was my experience. Everyone was trying to figure out what would happen next and what that would mean for *their* new realities. Needless to say, the overall transition forced me to stand alone and figure out my own next steps and new reality. I also had to learn to be okay by myself in the meantime. Whew! This part was undoubtedly uncomfortable, as I hadn't yet done the work in Chapter 8. However, my process afforded me opportunities where I learned to trust myself and I eventually learned to stand alone, which helped me to securely move forward towards creating a life that made me feel proud and authentic.

My journey to ending my toxic relationship with food was very similar. As I started to eat healthier and make better choices about what I put in my body, I began to lose weight as a result.

At the same time, I started noticing how people reacted and responded to the changes in my body and lifestyle. Instead of finally feeling included and accepted, which I thought would be the case if I lost weight, many times I just ended up feeling more like an outcast. The changes that I was making created shifts in my interactions with others, including those I was closest to. Sometimes the invites to dinner stopped and the gatherings where there was food became awkward. Some people started to assume that I would judge and critique their food choices and I was labeled the "health nut" and "food police." Who wants to hang out for dinner with this kind of person? No one and it showed.

I am not saying I didn't have friends and I didn't socialize with others during this time. But, what I am saying is that the separation and isolation became real. I had to learn how to continue on my journey alone, even if others were uncomfortable with it. Just as there were people who encouraged me to stay in my marriage because they thought it was best, there were people who told me that I didn't need to lose *that* much weight. I was told, "Slow down. Your head is getting too big for your body. Stop losing weight because you're going to look sick. You can stop going to the gym now." Losing more weight didn't make sense to these people. They were used to seeing me look a certain way and the changes didn't make sense in their minds. Early on in my weight loss journey, I was fortunate enough to realize that losing weight and making better food choices were my goals and I didn't need anyone's permission to pursue them. Reminding myself of this over and over helped me to continue my journey, especially when I didn't have others there with me.

It's Not About You; It's About Them

Humans are creatures of habit and familiarity. We like for our environments to stay the same without too much change, especially no quick changes. We need time to adjust; at least this is what we tell ourselves. However, life just doesn't work that way. In fact, when shifts in life happen, in most cases we don't have a lot of time to adjust. We just have to move! Having to move without much notice is one of the reasons many of us struggle in several areas of our lives, including weight loss and health. We're trying to adjust to a reality that may have changed (or is threatening to change) too quickly for us before we are ready.

Adjusting to a new lifestyle is hard and takes some work for you to catch up mentally. And, guess what? It's not just hard for you. It's hard for others as well. That's why it's not personal when those around you don't quickly adjust to your new lifestyle. It's not you with the problem. Those around you who say the harshest things or respond in negative ways are likely having a hard time accepting that change is happening. The reality is, when you change, their interactions with you will also change. You see, we don't just get antsy when change happens to us. We get antsy when change happens, period. So the next time someone tells you, "No, don't lose weight. I like you like this," what they're really saying is, "Stay how you are for me. I'm used to seeing you like this. How you look works for me." Again, it's not even about you; it's about them!

Grasping this perspective early on in your journey will save you a lot of confusion and feelings of betrayal and rejection. When others stop coming around and inviting you out, it is not a sign of rejection. It's just them sending you a message about their truth. They are not ready to change and they don't want to hang around you because you might be a reminder of that change that they're avoiding. Accepting this reality and adopting this perspective will also decrease emotional hang-ups and help you to move along on your journey alone if that's where you find yourself.

Once you stop listening to the voice of others and start listening to your own, you will be able to trust yourself a little more. Everyone will not understand your goals and where you're going. Everyone will not be okay with the changes you want to make. And, everyone will not want to go with you. That's good news! It's not for them anyway. While you will eventually need the support, learning to lean on yourself is an essential part of the process. After all, what helped me the most was learning to seek out people who supported me and learning to rely on myself regardless of whether that support was there or not.

Yes, in the previous chapter I told you to position yourself around people who have similar interests as you and to build that network. That's still the case; but, in the meantime, you might have to stand alone. If you've built trust in yourself as we talked about in Chapter 8, then you'll be just fine when those times come where you might be standing by yourself.

"Don't get mad when people don't show up for you, especially when you don't even show up for yourself."

- Dr. Ebony

Chapter 11

don't leave home without your goals

Would you be okay with sending your child to school every day to be taught by a teacher who never had any lesson plans or didn't follow through with his/her lesson plans? Would you be okay enrolling your child in a school where the principal didn't have a program for the school, its students, or its teachers? What if the principal and teachers told you on open house night that they were just going to wing the whole school year, would that be okay? I'm quite sure you wouldn't be okay with your child's educators "winging it" every day of the school year. Matter of fact, I can hear you telling me, "Hell no!" So, why is it okay for you to wing it when it comes to your own life and health? If winging it is not good enough for your child and their future, how has it become okay for you?

The most successful teachers, businesses, and programs are organized with plans and goals. Weekly meetings, quarterly performance reviews, and quality assurance teams are how these entities remain successful. On the flip side, some of the best and brightest ideas and businesses have fizzled due to a lack of planning, proper goal setting, and evaluation. Apparently, there's something to this whole planning and goal-setting thing! Wouldn't you agree? If you are still skeptical, let me share my own story.

From my own experiences, I've noticed that the times where I was most successful in life (i.e., getting into grad school, securing an internship, finishing grad school, and getting my first "real" job), I had specific plans, goals, and action steps. I took those same planning skills I had honed with my educational successes and applied it to my health journey. Why not? If it worked for those areas, surely it must work for health and weight loss too! Applying the same strategies from my most successful moments is how I've maintained an almost 14-year successful weight loss journey!

Now, it's your turn. It's time to apply your planning and goal-setting skills more broadly and stop limiting yourself and using those skills only when you're at work or parenting. I know you have been successful in life because of your ability to plan, set goals, and maneuver yourself through some of the most challenging situations. You haven't gotten this far in life without being good at planning, setting goals, and taking action steps! The promotions, jobs, juggling all of your duties, making sure your children get to their activities, taking care of others, and managing a household are all evidence that you are a badass when it comes to planning and setting goals! But, you have to believe that and start applying those same skills to losing weight and finally breaking up food.

When I started applying my skills of setting realistic goals to my health and weight loss journey, I was finally able to end my toxic relationship with food for good. Just like you, I vowed to leave the relationship many times in the past. I've even left a few times, but I always returned. I always went back when there were promises that things would be different this time. Things were never different. The relationship always remained the same. When I was tired of being sick and tired, I devised a plan, set some goals, and took the first step towards leaving for the last time. Having a plan and realistic goals helped me stick to my guns whenever I felt like I wanted to run back to that toxic relationship with food. To be honest, there were many times when it seemed much easier just to go back and deal with being unhealthy and overweight than to keep pushing along on a tough journey. Traveling an unknown journey, many times alone, was hard. However, my goals kept me motivated when I wanted to throw in the towel and gave me something new to always work towards. With proper goals and planning, I was never bored. There was always something different I could accomplish! But, I never would've reached this point if I hadn't started setting goals, re-evaluating those goals, and creating new action steps.

When breaking up with food, it is imperative that you have strategic goals and plans because they help you stay motivated and disciplined throughout your journey. It is likely that the way that you've set goals for your weight and health in the past will have to change, especially if they didn't work for you then. Your goals should be strategic, simple, direct, and time-limited. The problem that I see most often for people who fail on their health and weight loss journeys is that they devise broad, unrealistic, vague, and infinite goals with no strategy. For example, "I want to lose 100 pounds." This type of statement is not direct. It has no time limit. And, it's not a goal. It's a "want." A statement such as this lacks strategy and does not push you to take action, which is what makes a goal different than a want. A more strategic, realistic, direct, and time limited goal might be, "I will lose 100 pounds over the course of the next year. I will break down the weight loss into 25-pound increments every 3 months. I will lose 2 pounds a week, which is 8 pounds a month and 24 pounds by the end of 3 months." I suggest writing out this type of goal so that you can see it plainly and broken down. Such a goal is strategic – there is a long-term and short-term plan. It's direct – it tells you your exact target. It's realistic – you're not trying to tackle 100 pounds all at once, which is what most people do and become frustrated when it doesn't happen right away. Instead, breaking down a large weight loss goal into smaller goals is more realistic for the way life happens and the way your body responds to change. This type of goal is also time-limited. You're not just leaving it up to "whenever" for you to lose the 100 pounds. With this type of statement, you note the length of time you want it to take (one year), which is also realistic for that amount of weight loss. Next, there is a time limit provided for even the smaller weight loss targets. Setting the goals in 3-month increments give you the opportunity to go back and re-evaluate what you've done and to take a look at what went well as well as areas where you can improve.

Your next step is to start creating action steps to go along with those goals so that you can get moving towards making those changes happen and ending that toxic relationship with food. Some action steps might be getting a gym membership, reducing soda intake, reducing carb intake, setting appropriate bedtimes, drinking more water, reducing the number of times you eat out per week, etc. Your goals may remain the same many weeks at a time. That's okay. But, there are always a plethora of action steps to take to accomplish those goals! One week you might focus on drinking more water. The next week, you might focus on reducing the amount of sugar you use in your coffee. Nevertheless, there will always be something to work on to get you closer to your long-term goal of losing 100 pounds and breaking up with food.

Breaking up with food and losing weight is not something you can "wing." You've got to put in the work to plan to make sure that you're as successful as you can be. Planning keeps your health as a priority. It keeps you consistent. And, most of all, it keeps you motivated and excited to crush goals time and time again!

Chapter 12

do something different, if you

want something different

Although a little cliché, the saying that if you want something different, you have to do something different is true. I know you've heard it before but just stop and think I about it for a minute. Repeat it to yourself, even. If you want something different, you have to *do* something different. Let that sink in differently this time. Once it does sink in, you will realize that you cannot keep going about life the same way you've been doing and expecting (and, sometimes praying) to get new results. Continuing to engage in the same behaviors and expecting changes to fall into your lap is unrealistic. In essence, when you do this, what you are really expecting is a miracle.

Attempts to stay in your comfort zone may be the reason for repeating behaviors that you know haven't worked time and time again. Or, maybe you are hoping that it'll be different this next time. The truth is, it can be different. However, changes and results take work and work sometimes involves switching it up. I know you might be saying, "I have tried everything!" And, I hear you. Still, I want you to consider the thought that, yes, maybe you have tried a lot of things. But, have you tried changing aspects of YOU? Have you tried changing your way of thinking? Have you let go of being stuck in your ways? Or, are fear, frustration, and desperation leading you to search externally, instead of turning internally for the change?

Let's just say that you are afraid to change aspects of yourself because it moves you out of your comfort zone. Or, maybe you are beyond frustrated by a lack of change. To see the changes you want as it relates to your weight, health, and relationship with food, you're going to have to do something you haven't done before. And, more than likely, the change will have to start in you, especially with those toxic thoughts and words you say to yourself that continue to lead you back into those old habits and patterns with food and your weight. There's no way around changing this part. Change happens first in your mind and change cannot manifest in a toxic, static environment. If your mindset and statements to yourself are toxic, change will continue to be something you want instead of something you have. Feel free to go back to Chapter 6 where we discuss changing the mindset, as much is needed!

When it comes to relationships, whether it's with people, things, or food, carrying old habits into those new relationships rarely works out well. If you've ever tried to function in your old ways in a new relationship, chances are those same habits didn't work well, and you ended up getting the same results, just with a different person. That's what happens when you try to carry over the same habits into a new lifestyle. Although forming new patterns and seeking new ways of engaging with food and weight loss can be difficult, it is doable, and you're capable. Matter of fact, repeat this statement to yourself, "Change may be hard, but it is doable, and I am capable." Depositing positive statements such as these into your thought patterns is how you change your mindset and prepare it for the change you are seeking.

Once your mind is ready for change, the next step is taking a more in-depth look at the purposes that food serves in your life and in what capacity. Getting clear on how food works for you will help you find a realistic replacement and activity. Once you learn what can replace food in your life, you are starting down the path of doing something different other than eating yourself into ill health and continuing a relationship with food that hurts you more than helps you. Keep in mind; this is the time for you to be completely honest with yourself about how food serves you. Does it make you feel happy? Does food make you feel needed? Wanted? Does food soothe your loneliness or grief? Does food add excitement to an already stressful day? Whatever it is, let's get clear and honest. Now is not the time to say what you think I, or someone else, wants to hear. That's not going to help you with change. If food brings excitement to your already stressful day, then acknowledge that truth because when you choose to do something different, whatever you switch to doing will need to bring you that same level of excitement. Otherwise, it won't be a suitable, reliable replacement. And, it will not work long term.

After reading this chapter, I encourage you to write a list of all the ways that food serves you. I also encourage you to add to the list any emotions that food helps to reduce. Then, create a list of activities that can give you those same feelings and releases that do not involve food. For example, you can explore new places to go that are not food related. Or, you can discover new restaurants that have healthier food options. You might also find new groups that spark an interest in something you've always wanted to do. Having this type of list on hand will help you stay prepared when times come when you feel like you've tried everything and there is nothing left to try. We call this practice, planning ahead.

It is imperative that you prepare for those rough times and have a plan because they will come. You will want to go to your usual happy hour spot on Fridays when you've had a hard week. You will want to curl up on the couch and order your favorite take out when you're feeling lonely. All of these urges to go back to the familiar during stressful times is normal. However, when you're breaking up with food and trying to move on from that toxic relationship, you cannot afford to slip back because the risk that you will stay there is too high. Think about that relationship with that one person; when you tried to leave for good, the only way to ultimately move forward was to switch up your routine and your habits completely. You could no longer answer his/her phone calls and texts. You could no longer go to the same places you used to go where you would run into him/her. You could no longer have that casual sexual encounter…that is if you really wanted to move on. You know as well as I do that engaging in any of these behaviors, especially when times were hard, made it that much more difficult to really move on and get that person out of your system. Well, guess what? The same goes for that toxic relationship you have with food!

People ask me all the time how do they get rid of their sugar and food addictions. Although it might sound simpler than it really is, at the very basic level, you have to stop consuming it! You can't keep having intimate encounters with someone who you hope to get over. In the same way, you cannot keep indulging in sugar and expect to cease your sugar cravings and addictions. Every time you give in to the craving and indulge, the addiction grows stronger and is more persistent. If you're ever going to rid yourself of that toxic cycle and relationship with food, sugar, and even alcohol, you're going to have to stop doing what you used to and rearrange your life in a way that you don't rely on those old, familiar patterns to get you through. Instead, you develop new habits that renew your sense of self, control, power, and strength!

Completing the activity mentioned above might take some extra time, but do not neglect this exercise for the sake of keeping on with the book. Remember, to get something different, you have to be *willing* to do something different.

"Don't wait until you're desperate to make a change. Whenever you feel that nudge to do something different. Listen!"

- Dr. Ebony

"Goals are like a road map. They help you figure out where you're going when you've strayed off course."

- Dr. Ebony

Chapter 13

stop bouncing around

The two most common questions when it comes to dieting and eating better is, "Where do I start?" and "How do I stay consistent?" Beginning the process to end your toxic relationship with food requires that you first take inventory of your problem(s). Once you have identified the problem(s), then you are ready to devise a plan and resolution that directly addresses that issue. It would not be beneficial to your long-term goals to address other areas that are not problematic for you. For instance, if you are in a relationship where you experience frequent verbal abuse, it might not be beneficial to attend therapy because your partner does not clean up after him or herself. Instead, it would be more helpful for you to address the problem (i.e., verbal abuse) directly if you want a resolution to the abuse.

Unfortunately, many people begin their weight loss journey or process to change poor eating habits by not directly addressing the root problem(s). For example, if you struggled with late night snacking and overeating, it might not be beneficial for you to start your new journey with buying more weight equipment for your home. Sure, the weights might be helpful in the long run, but they do not directly address the persistent problem of late night snacking and overeating. Instead, it might be more beneficial to address why the late night snacking and overeating is happening in the first place (i.e., hunger, not eating enough throughout the day, insufficient water intake, emotional issues, stress, etc.). After this point, you can better target the core problem and create action steps to resolve it. First, identify your problem. Next, determine why the problem is there. Then, address ways to fix the problem(s). And, this is where you start!

Once you start with a program or regimen, the hardest part is staying consistent. We all know that it is easy to fall off of the wagon when you feel like you aren't accomplishing your goals. Or, you might stop if the process is not moving fast enough. Many times all it takes is that one step on the scale for you to become disappointed, frustrated, and return to your old habits. At other times you might even abandon the whole program because "it's not working" and switch to a new one before you ever see the program through to completion. Out of desperation, unrealistic expectations, and frustration, you start bouncing around and trying "everything" in hopes that something works. However, all you end up finding out, in the end, is that "nothing works." Does this sound familiar? If this sounds like you, chances are nothing is working because you are bouncing around and moving from program to program, which makes it nearly impossible for you to be consistent.

Consistency does not happen in a week or two or even a month many times. With processes like losing weight and changing your eating habits, you need to give a program and new regimen at least three months of consistency and healthy eating habits before you determine that it doesn't work. Realistic goals also need to accompany this 3-month "trial period." If you set your expectations to lose 75-100 pounds in 3 months, you're already setting yourself up for the program not to work. You also sabotage your ability to be consistent with such an unrealistic goal. Goals such as losing 20 pounds in three months are more realistic for some people and, therefore, help you to stay more consistent. Realistic goals give you an opportunity to see small changes happening, which, in turn, boosts your consistency.

The key to mastering your weight loss journey and creating a healthier relationship with food is mastering small areas, one at a time. Bouncing around from program to program (i.e., not eating meat, not eating carbs, juice diets, fasting, etc.) does not give you the chance to master anything before you are moving on to the next when the program doesn't work like you expect it to work. When you do this, you start to feel down on yourself and question your ability to succeed. When you stick with one program and tackle small areas at a time, you allow yourself to witness yourself being successful! Experiencing success might be eye-opening for you, especially if you usually view yourself as a failure or incompetent. Allowing yourself to observe your successes raises your confidence and consistency. Also, mastering one area before you move on to another will enable you to stack your achievements and victories so that you can refer to them down the road when the journey gets tougher.

It is almost impossible to build mastery when you are bouncing around from program to program. When you do this, you continue to build on your narrative that "nothing works." The more you start and stop and start and stop, the stronger that narrative becomes. You also start to beat yourself up and feel powerless in the process of weight loss and healthy eating.

In order for you to determine if something is working for you or not, give it all you've got for at least three months then re-evaluate your goals and progress, then decide whether you should move on or continue. This same principle is applied when you start a new job. A 3-month probationary period is typical. Companies do this for several reasons, with one main reason being the adjustment for both the company and the new hire. Companies know that adjustments can be rough and the fit might not be there. That's why they give the new hire a chance to see if it all works out. What if a company hired you and fired you after one week when you didn't bring in $100,000 revenue? That wouldn't be fair, would it? I didn't think so. But, you still apply the same type of unfair practices to your own health. It's unfair to yourself to quit before you've had a chance to adjust, work out the kinks, and learn from your mistakes.

Throughout this process of unlearning old habits and learning new ways of interacting with food, you're going to need to create as many moments as you can that lift your spirit, raise your confidence, and make you feel powerful and motivated. Learning to master different areas of your journey, one small victory at a time will do just that. No matter if you are seeking to up your water intake, eat more fruit, get more hours of sleep, go to the gym, or discontinue eating meat, starting with mastering one area at a time will help you remain consistent and is going to be key in your long-term success.

Chapter 14

notice the non-scale victories

We've all been conditioned by the weight loss industry to believe that the scale is the only way to tell if you're losing weight or not. Sure, the scale is important, but it's only one small piece of the bigger health puzzle. I'm here to help you undo the "brainwashing" that we've all been subjected to as it relates to the scale. It's time to unlearn what you have come to believe about the scale and the role that it plays in the bigger puzzle of you losing weight and adopting healthier eating habits. Most of us hold the scale as the sole determining factor in whether or not what we're doing is "working," which is why most weight loss efforts end in guilt and feelings of failure. In fact, if you're focusing on the scale as the determining factor of your success on your weight loss journey, then you're in for a long road of disappointment and frustration. Most of the frustration comes because you haven't learned that the process is more complex than the scale and comprised of other components that are just as important as the scale. I refer to those other elements as non-scale factors. And, when you are successful in tackling those elements, I call them non-scale victories.

Focusing on your non-scale victories more than the scale decreases your chances of feeling like a failure and feeling disappointed and guilty. Think about it; if you went into a relationship and only focused on one aspect of the other person, such as how much money he/she makes, you might be disappointed or leave the relationship when that person loses his/her job. When you do this, you neglect other aspects of the person such as how much he/she loves you, how he/she takes care of you, the protection he/she provides, the fun you have with the person, or the moments you share confiding in the person. As a consequence, you abandon an otherwise great partnership based on one aspect of the person's life and rob yourself of the chance to appreciate and experience all of the other goodness the person has to offer to you. Much of the same happens when you abandon your weight loss process when the scale doesn't say what you expect it to say. You leave an otherwise successful process before giving yourself credit for what you've done and reaping the benefits of your hard work.

When clients ask me for tips on how to stay motivated, one of the suggestions I give is to count non-scale victories. Counting non-scale victories broaden your mindset on what it means to lose weight. It allows you to take into account all of the things you are doing well! Many times when the scale doesn't move, there is the tendency to talk down to yourself and critique yourself for everything that you are not doing. However, when counting non-scale victories, you can pat yourself on the back for even the "small" things. After all, it's the small victories that create big change, increase your consistency, and keep you from falling off the wagon. Examples of non-scale victories are: making sure you have adequate water intake, meal prepping, going to sleep on time, decreasing soda intake, going to the gym when you said that you would, and making healthier choices when you eat out. Counting these non-scale victories helps you with your confidence, consistency, and motivation.

There is so much to work on in the weight loss process that dropping numbers on a scale is a tiny part of the entire picture. Most people get "bored" on their journey because they feel like either the food is boring, or they're tired of working on the same things. The truth is, if you work on mastering small areas of weight loss, one at a time, throughout of your journey, you will never get bored, and you will find that there will be several opportunities to count your successes. Being able to recognize your successes and victories, especially those not related to the scale, will make you feel more motivated, which will lead to more consistency and greater discipline. Having something to always work on and work towards provides you with more opportunities to master your process, instead of giving up time after time when what you're focusing on doesn't turn out as you hoped it would.

When I started focusing on non-scale goals like getting my workouts in, increasing my water intake, learning about healthier foods, and eating more frequently, I began to feel prouder of myself and critique myself a lot less than I did when I was just focusing on scale goals. Accomplishing my non-scale goals and counting those non-scale victories made me feel more confident, more powerful, and more in control. Since my scale doesn't move much these days as I am no longer "losing weight," counting my non-scale victories gives me the push I need to keep going when I want to give up on my journey or when I become frustrated with building a healthier relationship with food.

"Where you place your energy and priorities will determine what type of consistency you have…or, don't have."

- Dr. Ebony

Chapter 15

forgive yourself

Forgiveness is the conscious and deliberate choice of moving past negative feelings such as hurt, disappointment, betrayal, failure, and resentment. Forgiveness is intentional. The concept of forgiveness might be the hardest to grasp in life and the hardest strategy to implement on your health journey, but it's very necessary, and almost required! You will make mistakes and you will fall short of goals. Forgiveness is needed so that you have a level of compassion with yourself that enables you to get back up and keep pushing forward, instead of getting stuck in feelings of guilt, disappointment, and fear. However, forgiving yourself is hard because it means that you have to come to terms with some very harsh realities about yourself and your role in your relationship with food. In fact, this chapter might be a bit difficult to read because there are some harsh realities about yourself that we have to bring to light so that you're able to recognize and forgive yourself for the role that you've played in your toxic relationship with food.

All in all, forgiving yourself can be very hard, especially if you have formed the habit of it beating yourself up for your shortcomings and blaming yourself for life's mishaps. And while it might be a familiar place to be harshly critical of yourself, it can still be difficult to accept your role in where you are with regard to your health, weight, and relationship with food. But, you have a role in the toxic relationship that you have with food and you have to acknowledge and accept that truth before moving on to forgiveness.

I understand that you likely learned how to have a toxic relationship with food from your parents, family, and others around you. It is even more likely that the toxic relationship with food was passed down to you without you asking for it. Nevertheless, regardless of the origin of the relationship and how it landed in your lap, your job is to get yourself out of the toxicity before it takes you under! After all, you cannot keep blaming your parents, grandparents, and other people who took care of you for *maintaining* the current relationship you have with food. *You* did that. Although your interactions with food are probably automatic based on what you were taught, the truth is that you have some responsibility in the choices you make about your health. I do believe that you are doing the best you can with what you have. AND, accepting responsibility helps you remain accountable for your choices regarding your health.

Accepting responsibility is a hard pill to swallow, but it must be done in order to move forward to (and, through) the process of forgiveness. Owning your choices and taking responsibility for your role in the relationship provides space in your life for you to make necessary changes where they are needed. No one can do that but you. Since you cannot change anyone but yourself, acknowledging and accepting your role in your toxic relationship with food puts you on a path of corrective action and can decrease your resistance to the change process. If you focus on blaming someone or something else for where you have ended up, you can and never will change your situation. However, owning your role in it all gives you back your power to change the one and only thing you can change…you! This process of forgiveness renews your control over food!

What I've learned throughout my own experiences in life is that humans are the only species on Earth who punish themselves for a mistake or action over and over again. When a dog makes a mistake, they don't beat themselves up day after day. Instead, they carry on about their lives and live in the moment. Forgiving yourself lets you off of the hook and releases you from feelings of guilt, shame, and failure. The weight loss process is often filled with harsh critiques, comparing, nitpicking, and judgments. However, when you forgive yourself for your mistakes or shortcomings, you start the process of healing from that toxic relationship and ending the cycle of beating yourself up, being overly critical of your process, and comparing yourself to others. Forgiving yourself shows compassion, gentleness, and kindness to you, which is often missing in the weight loss process.

Be careful not to fall into the trap of using forgiveness as a means to justify and excuse your poor choices. The purpose of forgiveness is not to excuse or justify your poor choices related to your health. It is not a strategy you use when you want to rid yourself of your responsibility to stick to your goals. It is not something you rely on when you do not want to make better choices or when you lose motivation to stay the course. Instead, forgiveness is a tool of compassion that is most beneficial when you find yourself stuck in a place of guilt, shame, comparison, and negative self-talk as it relates to your health, weight, or food choices. Forgiveness does not give you permission to live in a mental space of denial and mindlessness. When you forgive yourself, you actually are creating a more positive, open, and empowering relationship with yourself and food. Forgiving yourself gives you a new level of understanding that helps you to get out of your own way and keep moving towards building a healthier relationship with food and, ultimately, yourself.

"Forgiveness is not optional for your success. It is required."

- Dr. Ebony

Chapter 16

create an attitude of gratitude

One of the most valuable conversations I have with my clients and others seeking to change their weight and health is the one about perspective. How you see yourself and the world around you will determine your emotional and behavioral responses in all aspects of your life, including your health journey. The timeless cliché, "perspective is everything," still holds true and is highly relevant to your weight loss journey. Ultimately, how you perceive your own efforts will make the difference between what you label a victory and what you call a failure.

Your perspective forms from what you learn, what you believe, and what you experience. It is unique to you and helps to shape your narrative about your life and the world around you. Several people can witness the same event, and all end up with different emotional reactions to the event as well as various narratives about what happened, why it happened, and what that means to them. Nonetheless, your perspective and your narrative can change. The change requires that you spend time challenging and ridding yourself of those thoughts and beliefs that you tell yourself over and over again and that have, consequently, kept you stuck. Statements of gratitude are a great way to begin to challenge faulty belief systems and old narratives that no longer serve you. Through my personal experiences and work with clients, I learned that when you engage in the practice of gratitude, in whatever form, your perspective begins to shift and you start to view yourself, your circumstances, and your possibilities in a fresh, new light.

The practice of gratitude, or being grateful, pushes you into a space where you can experience compassion and gentleness towards yourself. What you accomplish during your weight loss process and journey to building a healthier relationship with food will require that your perspective be that of continued gratitude. The space of gratitude is where you will be able to notice those small victories and be able to pat yourself on the back for even your most modest accomplishments instead of responding to yourself with familiar harsh criticism. People who ignore all other aspects of their weight loss journey but become frustrated because the scale doesn't say what they want it to say are not operating with an attitude of gratitude. Instead, their frustration is likened to praying for God to send you a husband or wife, then beating yourself up and becoming upset when the first relationship you get into doesn't result in marriage. Instead of expressing gratitude for discernment and God ending those situations that are not meant for you while also making room for your husband/wife to find you, you beat yourself up for being alone and begin with the narrative that you will always be alone and no one will ever want you.

Let's just be real, it's easier for us to gripe and complain about what we don't have, what we're not doing, and what's not working, rather than give thanks for what we do have, what we are doing, and what is working. Even if things seem like they are not going well for you at the very moment, an attitude of gratitude will shift your view from your current situation and turn your focus to the possibilities of what can be. You might be asking yourself what does an attitude of gratitude have to do with losing weight. It has everything to do with your weight loss process and the type of relationship you have with food! Remember, losing weight starts in your mind first, which will determine your perspective. If you perceive yourself as unable to accomplish your goals, you will be unable to accomplish your goals; that will be your constant reality and your attitude towards the process with be cynical and filled with skepticism. However, if you have an attitude of gratitude and express gratefulness for accomplishing your goals, even if they have not already come to pass, you invite that possibility into your reality, and you attract towards yourself the things you need to achieve the goal. In turn, you become intentional about your efforts and action steps. You become more mindful about how you go about your day and the food choices you make. You also begin to respond to your efforts with praise, positivity, and compassion, which then creates more motivation and consistency.

Within the last year, I have found this strategy to be absolutely invaluable and necessary! Creating an attitude of gratitude can take many forms – meditation, prayer, journaling, reading, etc. You have to find the method that works better for you and the one where you will be most consistent. For me, writing/journaling my statements of gratitude and, then, reading them aloud have helped me to stay consistent, mindful, motivated towards my goals. The goals that I wish to accomplish, whether they are in the present or future, are included when I write/journal statements of gratitude. I practice giving thanks for the goals I have already accomplished and those goals I wish to accomplish. For the goals I wish to accomplish, I write and speak about them as if they have already come to pass. This practice has been life changing not only for my health and training goals, but also for every aspect of my life including my businesses, relationships, finances, and emotions.

"This is your year of greatness. Remember, greatness takes time, diligence, and patience."

- Dr. Ebony

Chapter 17

reward yourself without food

I am a self-identified celebratory eater, which also makes me an emotional eater. I learned to reward myself with food during "good times" and celebrations. Also, early on in my journey, I rewarded my weight accomplishments with food. If I lost five pounds, that meant a celebration with food! After some time, this I realized that this cycle was stalling my progress. Therefore, to break my old ways of interacting with food and my old habits with emotional eating and rewarding myself, I intentionally practice being mindful about what I do in response to achieving goals, having happy feelings, and experiencing good times. Now, whenever something good happens to me, or I accomplish a goal, I try to catch myself and identify what I'm feeling. Once the emotion is identified, I determine what that emotion is urging me to do, which is usually to eat and drink. Next, I practice identifying my goal at the moment, "What am I trying to accomplish?" No matter my response, I ask myself, "Is this going to help me accomplish my goals? Will this reward or celebration with food keep me from my goals? If so, what else can I do that will be more helpful?" Having this type of dialogue with myself has helped me find other ways to reward myself and strengthen my ability to say no to food as the only way to celebrate and experience reward. Although turning away from food might not feel good in the moment, after I engage in a non-food activity and see myself making more progress towards my goals, I feel a sense of pride. I also feel powerful and in control of my journey!

For some reason, we've learned that the only way to reward yourself for doing well on your weight loss and health journey is with food. Contrary to popular belief, food is not the only way to reward yourself for sticking to and accomplishing your goals. If you're trying to end a toxic relationship with food, it seems counterintuitive that you would reward yourself with the very thing that you are trying to leave. Turning to food as a reward for "doing good" can also send you back into the space of emotional eating, especially if that's an area of struggle for you. For example, you feel proud or happy, which is an emotion, so you indulge in food as a result of those proud or happy feelings, thus, initiating a cycle of emotional eating. Eating in this way can be a slippery slope depending on your food choices and frequency of rewards. Let's face it; chances are the food that you are rewarding yourself with is not broccoli, kale chips, and chicken breasts.

Rewarding yourself with more unhealthy food for your victories is likely to put you back into the situation that has caused health and weight problems for you in the past. Take a personal relationship for example – if you were ending a toxic and unhealthy relationship with someone, you would not "reward" yourself for not talking to that person for five days by calling or texting them. If you feel like you have accomplished a major goal by not talking to the toxic person, you would not likely say, "Oh my! I haven't talked to him/her in three days. I'm so excited!

I'll reward myself by calling him/her." Or, "Oh my! He/she has been requesting to be intimate with me for two weeks, and I haven't given in! I'll reward myself by being intimate with him/her." That sounds absurd, right? Well, the same applies to rewarding yourself with food after accomplishing a goal related to ending your toxic relationship with food. Going back to the very thing that has kept you stuck, especially in the same familiar type of way does not push you forward on your journey. And, instead holds you back and leaves you at square one to start the process all over again.

Rewarding yourself and celebrating with food is one of those practices you, like myself, have made a habit from earlier years. It is as if we have been conditioned to believe that there is no other form of celebration other than that with food and drinks. It is important to remember that I am not advocating for no celebrations with food, ever! That is not realistic and definitely not the way I wish for you to live your life. The point I am driving home, however, is that turning to food as the *only* form of reward (like many of us do) does not help you on your journey to build a healthier relationship with food. Instead, it keeps you stuck and can make losing weight harder and more drawn out.

"Get comfortable with being uncomfortable."

- Dr. Ebony

The Healing Process

Chapter 18

getting closure & moving on

The relationships you find yourself in are up to you, especially those related to your food and health. Regardless of whether you learned to make poor food and health choices from your parents, grandparents, and others around you, your health is ultimately your responsibility. How you treat your body and what you allow in your body is your choice. Although I understand that education about and access to healthier foods is a huge barrier for many people, you have a responsibility to yourself, and your legacy, to do the best you can with creating the healthiest life you can with the resources that you have. The fact that you're reading this book is definitely a step in that direction and shows that you are taking back your power, gaining control over your health, and moving towards healing.

Just as with any other relationship that has ended, healing is a process and takes times. Healing from the end of a toxic relationship with food is not always going to be easy. In fact, it might be one of the hardest relationships you've ever left, yet the greatest reward that you've ever had! Some of those same strategies that you used to break up with food, including forgiveness and keeping an open mind, will be needed during the closure and healing process. The process of closure and healing from toxic relationships involves you making amends with your past conflicts (primarily internal conflicts), forgiving yourself for past (and, current) mistakes, and keeping an open mind to what your future holds as you move beyond your comfort zone and create healthier relationships.

Building a healthier relationship with food and healing does not mean that you cannot ever eat the foods that you love. In fact, it means the opposite. A healthier relationship with food puts you in the driver's seat and gives you control over whether you invite food along for the ride or not. And, if you decide to invite food along on the ride, that is because you *want* to and not because you feel like you have no other choice. That's the difference in being in a healthy relationship food and being in a toxic relationship with food. A healthy relationship with food does not leave you feeling powerless, critical, judgmental, and afraid. Instead, in a healthy relationship with food, you call the shots, you're in control, you feel empowered, and you have the power.

My hope to you as you move on in your healthier relationship with food is that you keep an open mind to the process, remain flexible, recognize your boundaries, and trust yourself and your efforts! Moving on and healing will not happen overnight and most certainly will not happen if you do not put forth some effort. Change is scary, but I am more than confident that just as you have done scary things before and succeeded, the same will happen for you as you end the toxic relationship with food that has kept you stuck and missing out on your greatness!

"You are right where you should be in life and have everything you need to start making the changes you want to see."

- Dr. Ebony

About the Author

Dr. Ebony & is Lifestyle & Weight Management Specialist and Food & Relationship Expert. She uses her background as a psychologist and own experience of losing over 50lbs to help women create healthier lifestyles and relationships with food. Dr. Ebony co-founded My Sister's Keep-her, LLC with her sister, Rhoda Ratliff, with a focus on providing services that help women recognize mindset and emotional barriers that keep them from achieving weight loss goals, maintaining a healthy weight, and ultimately in unhealthy relationships with food. Dr. Ebony is on a mission to reach women who struggle with an unhealthy relationship with food by motivating and creating change through emotional and mindset shifts. Dr. Ebony understands the underlying issues related to unhealthy weight and lifestyles and is here to help women figure it out and overcome what's been holding them back! The foundation of My Sister's Keep-her, LLC is to create a community of women helping each other become better and healthier. And, in turn, they create generational wellness and health. We are our sister's keeper!

Food Is Not Bae

Made in the USA
Monee, IL
15 April 2021

65817080R10079